A ROOKIE BIOGRAPHY

JACKIE ROBINSON

Baseball's First Black Major-Leaguer

By Carol Greene

CHILDRENS PRESS®
CHICAGO

This book is for Navada Nelson.

Jack Roosevelt Robinson (1919-1972)

LIBRARY OF CONGRESS
Library of Congress Cataloging-in-Publication Data

Greene, Carol.
    Jackie Robinson : baseball's first Black major-leaguer / by Carol Greene
        p.   cm. — (A Rookie biography)
    Summary: Relates the life story of the first black man to play baseball
in the major leagues.
    ISBN 0-516-04211-4
    1. Robinson, Jackie, 1919-1972—Juvenile literature. 2. Baseball
players—United States—Biography—Juvenile literature. [1. Robinson,
Jackie, 1919-1972. 2. Baseball players. 3. Afro-Americans—Biography.]
I. Title. II. Series: Greene, Carol. Rookie biography.
GV865.R6G74   1990
92—dc20
[796.357′092]
    [B]   89-28816
                                                       CIP
                                                       AC

Jack Roosevelt Robinson
was a real person.
He lived from 1919 to 1972.
He was the first black man
to play baseball
in the major leagues.
This is Jackie's story.

TABLE OF CONTENTS

The house on Pepper Street

Chapter 1

Pepper Street

Crack! went the bat
on the ball.
Off went Jackie.
He was the smallest kid
in the neighborhood.
But he could play ball.

All five Robinson
children liked sports.
They helped one another.
That was what Mama
wanted them to do.

The family lived
in a house on Pepper Street
in Pasadena, California.

Sometimes white neighbors
were mean to them
because they were black.

But Mama stayed calm.
She taught her children
not to be afraid.
She took them to church
and told them to be kind.

The Robinson family lived in Pasadena, California.
Jackie is second from the left.

Mallie Robinson
was Jackie's mother.

Every day, Mama went
out to do housework.
Jackie's father had gone away.
So Mama had to earn money.
Sometimes all they had to eat
was bread and sugar water.

As Jackie grew older,
he got a paper route.
He cut lawns
and ran errands too.
He wanted to earn
money for his mother.

Then Jackie joined
the Pepper Street gang.
They stole things
and threw dirt at cars.
Jackie seemed to be headed
for big trouble.

But a wise neighbor,
Carl Anderson, talked to him.
He told Jackie
he would hurt his mother
by getting in trouble.

Mr. Anderson said it wasn't brave
to do bad things
just because the gang did.
It was brave *not* to do them.
Jackie listened to him.

Jackie also listened to
the Reverend Karl Downs,
a minister at his church.
Karl Downs liked kids.
He helped Jackie a lot.

So Jackie turned to sports.
He got better and better.
In high school, he earned
letters in football, baseball,
basketball, and track.

Then he began to dream.
Maybe his sports would
win him a scholarship
to a big university.

Chapter 2

Old Dreams,
New Dreams

Jackie's dream didn't
come true right away.
For two years, he
went to Pasadena
Junior College.

Jackie was a
basketball star
at Pasadena
Junior College.

He helped make the college
a champ in football,
baseball, and basketball.
Then the scholarships came.
Jackie chose UCLA
because it was near home.

Soon Jackie had letters
in four sports again.
No one had done that
before at UCLA.
He also was chosen as
an all-American halfback.

Jackie was a football star at UCLA (University of California, Los Angeles)

At UCLA, Jackie met
a girl, Rachel Isum.
She was studying
to be a nurse.
Before long, she was
the only girl for Jackie.

But Jackie still worried
about his mother.
He still wanted
to earn money for her.
So he quit school.

Today, he could have
earned a lot of money
playing professional sports.
But back then,
blacks couldn't do that.

So Jackie worked with kids and sports.
He played some semipro
football on the side.
Then, in 1942,
the army drafted him.

In 1942,
Jackie was
drafted into
the army.

Lieutenant Robinson

Jackie was smart.
He became an officer.
The army asked Jackie
to play on a football team.
But some other teams
wouldn't play a team
with a black person on it.

So Jackie quit football.
He asked to join
an army baseball team.
He was told he must
play on a black team.
There was no black team.

Jackie had many problems
like that in the army.
At last he got out.
He wanted to marry Rachel.
But he needed a job.

In those days, blacks
could not play baseball
in the all-white major leagues.
They had to play
in the Negro League.

Jackie played
for the
Kansas City
Monarchs.

So Jackie joined
the Kansas City Monarchs.
Then one day in 1946,
he got a strange message.
A man called Branch Rickey
wanted to talk to him.

Chapter 3

A Pro

Branch Rickey was president
of the Brooklyn Dodgers.
He once saw a black college player
turned away from a hotel.
Rickey got the black player
a cot in his room.

That night he watched
the young player cry.
Rickey never forgot
that. He wanted to
change things.
This was his chance.
Rickey talked to Jackie.

Branch Rickey asked Jackie
to play for the Brooklyn Dodgers.

He would make Jackie
the first black player
in major-league baseball.
He knew Jackie was good.
But he would have to be brave too—
very brave.

Rickey told Jackie that
people would yell and
call him ugly names.
Players might hurt him.
But Jackie must never fight back.
If he did, he could ruin things
for other black players.

When Jackie signed his contract with the
Dodgers, he became the first African American
to play in the major leagues.

Jackie and Rachel shortly after their wedding

Jackie said yes.
He and Rachel got married.
Then he went to play
with the Dodgers'
farm club in Montreal, Canada.

In his first game,
Jackie hit a three-run homer.
He played great ball all year.
Montreal fans loved him.
But others yelled their hate.

Jackie never fought back.
That year, his team won
the Little World Series.
Now he'd be a Dodger.
He would play in the major leagues.

Manager Ben Chapman of the Philadelphia Phillies meets Jackie in 1947.

His first Dodger game
was on April 15, 1947.
Jackie didn't play well.
Some of his own teammates
didn't want him.
It was a hard time.

Jackie was soon accepted by the Dodgers as part of the team.

Then other teams screamed
at him from their dugout.
The Dodgers didn't like that.
After all, Jackie was *theirs*.
So they became a real team.

Ford Frick was president
of the National League.
He told other teams that
Jackie had a right to play.

Ford Frick later gave Jackie
the silver-bat award for
winning the National League
batting title.

Jackie scores on a home run.

From then on, Jackie
played like a star.
He shone at second base.
He hit .297 and led
the league in stolen bases.

Jackie slides toward home plate.

That year, the Dodgers
won the pennant
and Jackie Robinson
was named Rookie of the Year.

Chapter 4

Baseball Years

Jackie's problems weren't over.
Fans still yelled at him
because he was black.
Sometimes he and Rachel
had trouble finding a house.
But good things happened too.

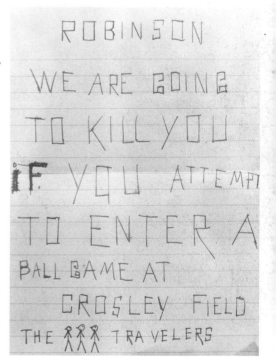

Jackie answered this hate letter by
hitting a home run in the next game.

Once Jackie yelled at an umpire.
The ump threw him out—
but not because he was black.
He treated Jackie
like "just another guy."
That made Jackie feel great.

Ford Frick gave Jackie the award for Most Valuable Player of 1949.

He kept playing well too.
In 1949, he was named
Most Valuable Player
in the National League.

Soon other blacks joined
major-league teams.
Branch Rickey said that
Jackie had done his job.
Now he could fight back.

Jackie surrounded by some of his trophies

Jackie was active in the
civil rights movement.
In the 1960s, he marched
and picketed for racial
justice. Opposite page:
In 1970, Jackie attended
an anti-drug block
party in Harlem, New York.

Jackie did.
He talked in many places
about unfairness to blacks.
He made some people mad.
But he knew he was right.

At his birthday party in 1949, Jackie, Jr., was a happy three year old.
Unfortunately, his teen years were not happy.

He and Rachel had three children,
Jackie, Jr., Sharon, and David.
Jackie even starred in
a film about his life,
The Jackie Robinson Story.
And he played and played.

Rachel and Jackie, Jr., visit with actor Dick Lane (above)
on the set of *The Jackie Robinson Story*. Jackie, who played
himself in the movie, is seen below with Rachel (center) and actress Ruby Dee.

Jackie's great work at second base
helped the Dodgers win the World Series in 1955.

In 1955, the Dodgers
won the World Series.
Jackie said that was
"one of the greatest
thrills of my life."

Then in 1957, he retired.
He was almost 39.
That was old for baseball.
But Jackie still had
plenty of work to do.

Jackie, Jr., helped his father "hang up his glove" when Jackie retired from baseball.

Chapter 5

"I Never Had It Made"

Jackie became vice president
of a company called,
Chock Full O'Nuts.
He also traveled around
and raised money
to help other African-Americans
fight unfairness.

Jackie supported the integration marchers in St. Augustine, Florida, in 1964.

He liked business
and he liked politics.
He helped some people
run for office.
He also became friends with
Dr. Martin Luther King, Jr.

Jackie worked for
Hubert Humphrey,
the Democratic
candidate for president
in 1968.

Jackie and Dr. Martin Luther King, Jr. (above), received honorary law degrees from Harvard University. Below, Jackie talks with James Farmer (in light suit) before a civil rights march.

Jackie was the first black player elected to the Baseball Hall of Fame.

In 1962, Jackie was elected
to the Baseball Hall of Fame.
He had a lifetime
batting average of .311.

Jackie presents a check to Arthur Spingarn of
the NAACP for the "Fight for Freedom Fund" drive.

He also helped start
the Freedom National Bank
in Harlem, New York City.
It was owned and run
by black people.

The Robinson family in 1962. From left to right,
Rachel; Jackie, Jr.; David; Sharon; and Jackie.

But Jackie had hard times too.
In 1965, Branch Rickey died.
in 1968, Jackie's mother died.
Jackie missed them both.

Then there was Jackie, Jr.
He had trouble being
the son of a famous man.
He got mixed up with drugs.

At last he broke his habit.
He began to help other users.
But in 1971, he was killed
in a car accident.
That almost broke Jackie's heart.

Early in 1972, the Dodgers
retired Jackie's number.
No other Dodger could
ever wear number 42.
Then, in October of 1972,
Jackie Robinson died.

David Robinson assists his mother at Jackie's funeral. On the right is the Reverend Jesse Jackson, who spoke at the funeral.

Jackie in his Dodger uniform, attending a movie premiere
with Rachel, and reading the Sunday comics to his children

In the last picture taken of him, Jackie throws out
the first ball at a World Series game in 1972.

He had done so much.
But he once said,
"I never had it made."

He felt that he never
would have it made
as long as one
African-American person
was still unfairly treated.

45

Important Dates

1919   January 31—Born in Cairo, Georgia, to Mallie and Jerry Robinson

1920   Moved to Pasadena, California

1939   Went to UCLA

1946   Married Rachel Isum

1947   Played first game for the Brooklyn Dodgers Named National League Rookie of the Year

1949   Named Most Valuable Player in the National League

1957   Retired from baseball

1962   Elected into Baseball Hall of Fame

1964   Helped start Freedom National Bank

1972   October 24—Died in Stamford, Connecticut

INDEX

Page numbers in boldface type indicate illustrations.

PHOTO CREDITS

ABOUT THE AUTHOR

Carol Greene has degrees in English literature and musicology. She has worked in international exchange programs, as an editor, and as a teacher. She now lives in St. Louis, Missouri, and writes full-time. She has published more than eighty books. Others in the Rookie Biographies series include *Benjamin Franklin, Pocahontas, Martin Luther King, Jr., Christopher Columbus, Abraham Lincoln, Robert E. Lee, Ludwig van Beethoven, Laura Ingalls Wilder,* and *Daniel Boone.*